A TEACHER'S GUIDE TO

USING HISTORIC HOUSES

Gail Durbin

English # Heritage

CONTENTS

ENGLISH HERITAGE

The Link Building, Chiswick House.

ABOUT THIS BOOK

There cannot be many schools in England more than 30 miles from a historic house which is open to the public. This book is intended to help teachers who plan to take their pupils on a visit. It starts by providing some historical background to show how the layout of historic houses was altered over time as a response to changes in their function and use. Ways of looking at empty and ruined buildings are provided as well as suggestions for dealing with the more common furnished house. Some of the most useful visual and written sources are covered and issues relating to the historic house today are addressed. The book includes a list of further resources.

The historic house is defined as any building put up in the past as a home, and the book covers houses from the medieval period onwards. The specific houses mentioned in this book were diverse in ownership, household size, and social purpose. This book does not deal exclusively with the country houses which reflect the lives of a limited stratum of society, although examples are drawn principally from buildings in the care of English Heritage. Since many of these have been preserved for their architectural merits rather than because they represent the homes of a cross-section of society, the book is necessarily biased towards the upper end of the social scale. Many of the approaches suggested could equally well be applied to your pupils' own homes with interesting results.

Chiswick House, London.

UNDERSTANDING HISTORIC HOUSES

In the past two decades there has been a movement away from studying buildings simply in terms of space and style in favour of understanding how they were actually used. Houses reflect the social organization and aspirations of the society that produced them, and this chapter shows how a study of a house can be used as historical evidence to illuminate the period when it was built and used.

Social status may derive from respect for the individual or for the post or position that he or she holds, and it can be bolstered by the accumulation of impressive possessions. Large houses have always been status symbols and gradually the objects that filled them began to perform that role too. The ways in which a building and its furniture were used to focus on and enhance the status of its owner is another theme of this chapter.

THE EARLY MEDIEVAL HOUSE

A good example of an early medieval house is Old Soar, at Plaxtol in Kent, built about 1290 as a small manor house. There was once a hall 13m x 10.25m open to the rafters and at the end of this, reached by a stone spiral staircase, was a private room for the lord's family, known as a chamber.

The hall was the centre of secular life in the medieval manor, and symbolised the fine social balance of obligation and responsibility that held communities together when there was no guarantee of strong national government. Many early houses show signs that there was no complete confidence in any lasting peace. At Old Soar the loops (or arrow slits) in the wall at ground floor level show that people were prepared for unsettled times. The lord protected his people; he offered justice, shelter and peace, and in return he expected loyalty, and service – in the form of fighting men if necessary but generally in the form of agricultural labour. He could not maintain his position without the willing support of the people on his estates and they in turn had a vested interest in the security that his strength provided.

This interdependence and unity was reflected in the hall where life was lived communally. Just as people on the manor estate needed to work collaboratively so emphasis was placed on communal living rather than separation and privacy. The hall was used for eating, sleeping and entertainment. Its physical size dominated the manor and the provision of hospitality symbolised the pivotal role of the lord in his manor. The lord could, however, withdraw from the hall to his private quarters in the chamber from where he was able (literally) to oversee events in the hall through a peep-hole.

Private accommodation at this date was seldom elaborate. At Old Soar it consisted of the chamber, a second room containing a garderobe (or latrine), and a chapel. Rooms were used collectively by the family and were not highly specialised in function so that the chamber approximated to a bed-sitting-room. Furniture was probably very limited. Although it later became an important status symbol, furniture played a minor role in underpinning the social position of the lord, and even royal palaces were left empty of furniture when the court moved on – a custom which continued into the seventeenth century.

The chamber, Old Soar.

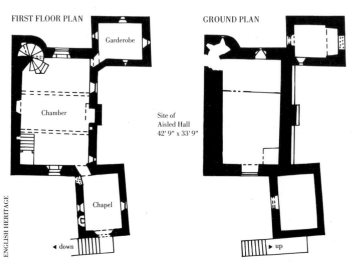

FIRST FLOOR PLAN

GROUND PLAN

Garderobe

Chamber

Chapel

Site of Aisled Hall 42' 9" x 33' 9"

◄ down

► up

Ground floor and first floor plan of Old Soar, Plaxtol, Kent.

THE LATER MEDIEVAL HOUSE

Built in the mid fifteenth century, Gainsborough Old Hall in Lincolnshire is a fine example of a late medieval manor house. The hall itself is impressive and was served by a range of kitchens and stores, known as domestic offices. It was still the centre of the manor but, with increasing wealth and the subdivision of household functions, the number of private apartments increased. From the second half of the fourteenth century, the lord left the hall to his household whilst he withdrew to his more private apartments and appeared in the hall only for major occasions.

ENGLISH HERITAGE

Gainsborough Old Hall looking towards dais.

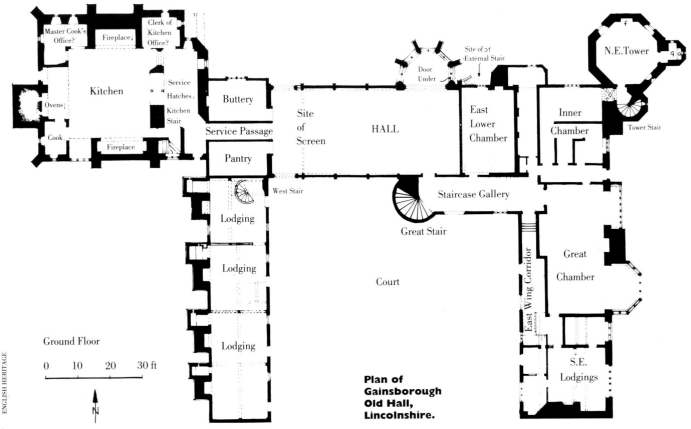

ENGLISH HERITAGE

Plan of Gainsborough Old Hall, Lincolnshire.

Gainsborough Old Hall demonstrates the classic arrangement of a late medieval hall. The hall itself was large so that the whole household could be seated to eat, and it was heated by a fire in the centre. The wood smoke found its way out through a louvre in the roof. The lord's end of the hall was given status by the provision of a raised platform or dais for the high table, and the building enhanced his status further by the addition of an elaborate bay window, known as an oriel window, to the side of the dais to provide light for the lord and his guests. Sometimes there was also a canopy on the wall behind the lord.

At the opposite end of the hall three doors gave access to the buttery, where wine and ale were stored, and the cellar and the corridor to the kitchens. Large medieval houses were more like a collection of buildings than a single block. This arrangement allowed the kitchen to be separate reducing the hazard of fire. It also meant that the corridor leading to the centre door at the end of the hall could serve a ceremonial function and allowed food to be paraded into the hall towards the lord. This is a further example of the design of the building being used to focus attention on the lord and underpin his position.

The proliferation of different domestic departments or offices was another sign of increasing specialization within the lord's household. Each area was presided over by an official with apartments with one or two rooms, each with their own fireplace and garderobe. The pattern was repeated on a grander scale in royal palaces such as Hampton Court and Eltham.

ENGLISH HERITAGE

create more counter space. Beneath the house was a cellar where goods, especially wine, were stored. Apart from these clearly commercial areas the rest of the house functioned, and therefore had the same elements, as the house of any moderately wealthy man. The middle section was a hall, open to the roof as an indication of status, where employees could be fed and guests entertained. Behind this was a private room. It was clearly an important room because the ceiling joists and wallposts are elaborately moulded and there is a separate fireplace. Above were two bedchambers. The kitchen was probably a separate building in the yard outside where there was also a latrine pit.

Cutaway drawing of the Medieval Merchant's House, Southampton, as it has been restored.

specific responsibilities. The butler in the buttery was responsible for the butts of wine and ale and for the provision of candles. The pantler was responsible for the pantry where bread was stored. The cellarer was responsible for dry provisions, and in the kitchen the cooks were supervised by the steward.

The private apartments at Gainsborough Old Hall were reached by a small spiral staircase behind the dais. By the late middle ages the role of the chamber had changed and it came to be called the great chamber. Generally the great chamber was on the first floor and might occasionally be used for entertainment. As the room became more important so it became more elaborate. At Longthorpe Tower, Lincolnshire, the chamber was decorated in the fourteenth century with extensive wall-paintings showing biblical and secular scenes.

Hospitality was still an important obligation in later medieval society and it was common for large medieval houses to be built with lodgings to accommodate guests, accompanied by their own personal households. Lodgings often took the form of sets of self-contained

Wall-painting in the chamber at Longthorpe Tower, Cambridgeshire.

Medieval Merchant's House, 58 French Street, Southampton, is a more modest house. Now restored to what it might have looked like in the early fourteenth century, it too reflects in its design the purpose it was intended to serve. In this case it was a combined shop, store, and home of a prosperous merchant. The front room at ground level was a shop, and shutters on the street front let down to

THE TUDOR AND JACOBEAN HOUSE

Kirby Hall, in Northamptonshire, was originally built in 1570 for a leading courtier of Elizabeth I and its plan reveals social organization which was still of the medieval type.

The gateway creates an impressive entrance and the inner court is flanked on two sides by lodgings. The entrance into the house proper, emphasized by an elaborate porch, takes the guest straight into the great hall which in this case has a gallery (of later date but probably replacing an earlier one) suitable for housing a small band of musicians.

The doorway under this gallery gave access to the usual range of domestic offices: the buttery, the cellar and the kitchens. The great hall has a fireplace in the side wall and the whole room was originally lit from two sides by huge glass windows. The private apartments have been obscured by later rebuilding, but we know a new type of room, a long gallery, was built.

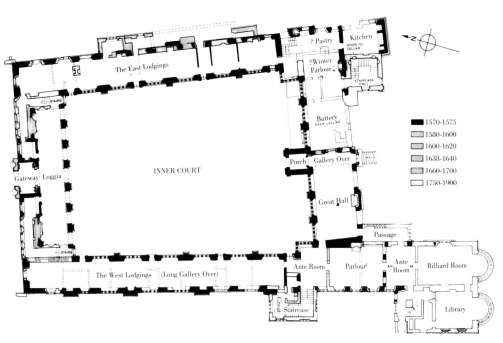

■	1570-1575
▨	1580-1600
▧	1600-1620
▤	1638-1640
▥	1660-1700
□	1750-1900

Kirby Hall, Northamptonshire.

Later additions to the house between 1575 and 1591 are significant. The grand nature of the great staircase to the upper floor makes it clear that the great chamber was no longer a private room but one of the principal rooms for entertaining. Other more private rooms were also built which reflect the needs of changing behaviour patterns. Close contact between the owner of the house and his retainers was no longer necessary. An increasingly stable society meant that the lord did not rely so heavily on them for physical support in time of disturbance. Increasing wealth meant that services could be bought instead of exchanged as they had been in the

7

earlier symbiotic relationship between lord and people. Home life became more relaxed and private. The lord could afford to withdraw further from the servants and an increased desire for privacy is apparent in the new range of rooms. An informal room, the parlour, appears, which in smaller houses may sometimes have doubled as a guest bedroom. This separation spread down the whole household so that by the early seventeenth century upper servants might have their own parlour. The provision of a library reflects the changing role of a gentleman from soldier to scholar.

Gardens were valued in Tudor times and in the late sixteenth century intricate knot gardens developed and were established below the windows of the lord's private rooms. In the following century the knot garden expanded into the parterre with its larger scale and flowing patterns. Gardens are ephemeral things with complex histories but in recent years excavation has been used to identify the extent of beds and paths, and seed and pollen analysis has helped fill out the detail of the planting, so that tentative reconstructions can be made. An example is the parterre at Kirby Hall.

THE FORMAL HOUSE 1630-1720

A visit from the monarch was the ultimate social accolade, bringing with it the likelihood of further preferment but also enormous financial outlay. Hopeful courtiers prepared formal suites of rooms, known as state apartments, that copied the royal palaces in their layout.

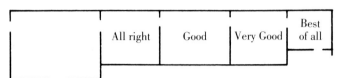

The relative status of the rooms in an apartment.

It is important to grasp the concept of an apartment because it was a key feature in the design of large houses until the early eighteenth century in England. It consisted of a self-contained sequence of rooms, one opening off the next with no corridors in between. It might be occupied by the owner or a guest, and a large house might have several apartments. The sequence might be made up of an ante-room which was a fairly public room, a withdrawing room which was a private sitting room, a bedchamber

which could also perform the role of sitting room, and a closet which was a small intimate private room where the owner might keep collections or other valued possessions. The closet might also house the close stool or commode which had superseded the latrine as the normal form of sanitation.

The length of the sequence of rooms in an apartment might differ with the importance of the occupant. In royal palaces or houses where the monarch was expected there might also be a presence or great chamber where the king could conduct public business.

The etiquette associated with the use of apartments reflected social hierarchies and provided great opportunity for power play. Since each room in the sequence was more private than the previous room, how far a visitor penetrated into the sequence in

Audley End House, Essex.

ENGLISH HERITAGE

someone else's apartment was determined by his or her status and degree of familiarity and intimacy with the occupant. Only intimate friends would have been invited into the closet.

At Audley End, in Essex, Thomas Howard, Earl of Suffolk, prepared matching state apartments for the king and queen in anticipation of a royal visit in about 1610. They were planned in the classic manner on the first floor of an inner court with the family apartments below and the servants on the second floor or in the outer court. The relative status of the different accommodation is made obvious from the outside by the differing heights of the storeys and the window size.

By now the great hall was presided over by a servant with the title of steward and was either merely an eating place for servants or was used for festivities in which aristocracy and servants both took part. Further evidence of the increasing separation of lord and servants is the backstairs that served each of the major apartments and allowed servants to perform their tasks discreetly, unseen by the master.

The formal house was complemented by a formal garden with straight avenues, canals and walks. Just as the building focused attention on the owner so also the garden worked in the same way, with the principal paths and vistas radiating out from the main room of the house.

THE EIGHTEENTH-CENTURY HOUSE

The formality of the seventeenth century gave way to the more relaxed social life of the eighteenth century. Security was no longer a major factor and entourages were smaller. A way of demonstrating wealth and status was the giving of large balls and parties. Unlike the previous century, when it was expected that everyone would move on to the next phase of the entertainment together, in the eighteenth century a number of activities would take place simultaneously, so there might be cards in one room, music in another, and a running buffet elsewhere.

Private apartments were unsuitable for this form of entertainment and new fashionable houses were designed on a circular plan so that if necessary the whole floor could be used. Sometimes the bedchamber was removed from this route to an upper floor although the presence of a bed in a public room would not have been the subject of comment as it would today. As people spent more time in the public rooms so the need for apartments diminished and guests instead would be provided with a bedroom and a dressing room which was also used as a sitting room.

Marble Hill House, in Twickenham, built between 1724 and 1729 for Henrietta Howard, mistress of George II, is a good example of this design of house. It was built on a small scale as a summer retreat from London. The house was designed as a

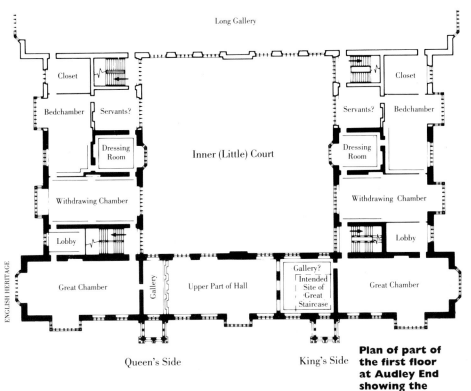

Plan of part of the first floor at Audley End showing the arrangement of the state apartments.

Paths and hedges radiate from a central point in Chiswick House grounds.

block with a connected domestic wing (since destroyed). The entrance, at ground floor level, is into a pillared but low hall which takes the form of a lobby. Except when they acted as attendants the servants had by now been banished altogether from the hall into the domestic wing or to attic dormitories. The housekeeper, however, had a bedroom on this floor, and, since the main room was no longer used for eating, separate eating rooms were included.

Most of the main rooms, however, were still on the first floor. An impressive mahogany staircase took visitors up to the great room, mirrored and gilded, that could not fail to impress. The other rooms on this floor were bedrooms and a dressing room, but in times of need the connecting doors would have been opened and they would have become public rooms. A single set of backstairs was considered sufficient.

The symmetrical arrangement of the rooms and the furniture within them reflected the pursuit of order and balance in society. There was still not a great deal of furniture in use but the innovation was that it was often designed especially for the house. The great eighteenth-century

architect Robert Adam designed carpets to reflect the design of his ceilings. They finished short of the edge of the room so that the border was not broken into by the furniture arranged against the walls. When needed the furniture would be drawn forward and later replaced. For this reason decoration seldom found its way onto the reverse side of chair backs since the only people likely to see this part were the servants. At the beginning of the eighteenth century dining-tables too were kept folded, or in pieces, in corridors, and only brought out when needed.

The circular arrangement of the house influenced garden design. Views and vistas were no longer created to be seen from the principal apartment but surprise features were planned to be viewed from several positions, and it became fashionable for guests to be taken on a circuit of the grounds. The English enthusiasm for landscape gardening led to the sweeping away of flower beds, avenues and canals, and an emphasis on winding lakes, curved lines, clumps of trees, and contrived naturalness punctuated by classical temples. The most famous of gardeners, Capability Brown was

employed to improve upwards of 150 gardens including those at Appuldurcombe House, Audley End and Wrest Park. Humphry Repton succeeded him but created a different type of garden. He revived the flower-garden on the terrace and aimed to replicate the ruggedness of nature rather than Brown's tamed view.

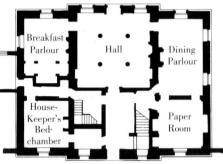

Ground Floor

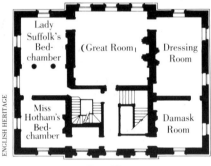

First Floor

Plan of Marble Hill House.

Marble Hill House, London.

THE NINETEENTH-CENTURY HOUSE

Late eighteenth-century romanticism brought an increased desire to be in touch with nature. Desire for informality led to houses being built in asymmetrical designs and some of the rigid room layouts of earlier periods disappeared. For this reason it is less easy to predict the arrangement of a house. Some trends are apparent though. The principal rooms of a house were often to be found on the ground floor, as compared to the first floor as in earlier times, so that the windows and doors could be thrown open to the garden. House parties became popular and specialized areas were provided within the house for the entertainment of guests. Billiard rooms, music rooms and studies were added, whilst furniture was arranged in intimate groups to encourage conversation.

Osborne House, on the Isle of Wight, built in 1845-46, is a classic example of a Victorian country house even though royal ownership necessitated some extra formal rooms. The family accommodation was self-contained and the servants were housed in a separate wing. The main rooms on the ground floor had easy access to the terrace and gardens. The house was built with a water supply available on all floors, flushing lavatories, and a hot air central heating system. As in other Victorian houses increased wealth and the division of labour was reflected in the servants' working accommodation where every separate domestic function was allotted, where possible, an individual space of its own. In the basement at Osborne there were rooms devoted to upholstery, lamp cleaning, wine storage, and silver cleaning. The 'hall' had become either the servants' hall or the place for entertaining tenants at Christmas.

The Victorian house reflected the moral code of the period by paying particular attention to the sleeping quarters of both servants and guests. Better servants' bedrooms were provided. The servants' dormitory disappeared in favour of having no more than two or three people to a room. Single male and female guests were sometimes separated by positioning their accommodation at either end of the house and bachelors might expect fairly spartan bedrooms. Nineteenth-century gardens were as varied in their style as the architecture of the period. Osborne House had an Italianate terrace with fountains, balustrades, statues and formal planting. Carpet bedding, which still survives in many municipal parks, used annuals to create dense and intricate planting whose colours and patterns reflected contemporary taste in interior decoration. At Belsay Hall in Northumberland, on the other hand,

ROYAL COMMISSION ON THE HISTORICAL MONUMENTS OF ENGLAND

**Belsay Hall
quarry gardens,
Northumberland.**

a natural style was developed in the dramatic quarry gardens. The addition of tennis and croquet lawns reflect late Victorian leisure interests.

Once you have grasped the method and value of analysing a house in terms of the relationship between layout and use then you can look at all structures in the same manner to try to squeeze from them some of their history. It is possible, for example, to apply the same method to a Victorian terraced house or a modern Wimpey house.

In the Wimpey house plan the hall is too small to contain much furniture suggesting that it has become no more than a passageway. The bedrooms, bathroom and lavatory on the upper floor all open onto the landing space, not each other, suggesting that these are all seen as private areas. The relative size of the bedrooms reflects a hierarchy, but all occupants have equal access to the bathroom and lavatory. Downstairs the interconnecting sitting room and dining room form the largest space in the house and have the largest windows, indicating that this is the most social and prestigious area.

The interconnected sitting room and dining room suggest that there is no longer a clear division between these two activities. The kitchen is well fitted suggesting that much time will be spent there or that the activity is accorded status.

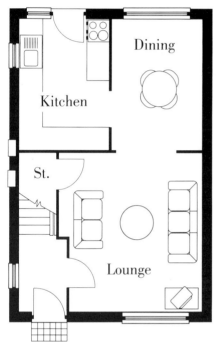

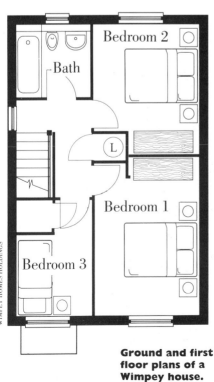

WIMPEY HOMES HOLDINGS

**Ground and first
floor plans of a
Wimpey house.**

ASKING QUESTIONS

Architectural historians making a study of a building generally start with the outside and examine it closely to see what can be discovered and what problems it throws up. They look for signs of different phases of building and then make a careful study of the inside to see if any of the problems observed outside can be answered. Going through this process is easier in an empty house because you can avoid the distraction of the furnishings which may tell a different story. It might help you to organize your study if your pupils are trained to ask a series of structured questions.

Outside

■ Why was this house built here?
- defence, landscape, location, fashion, availability of land

■ What building materials have been chosen? Why?
- availability, fashion, defence, climate, economic status

■ Have there been any alterations to the outside?
Removals? Why?
- disaster, redundancy, fashion, deterioration, cost
Additions? Why?
- fashion, new needs, increasing wealth, status symbol

■ What style has been chosen? Why?
- tradition, defence, fashion, newness, character of building material

Inside

■ How do you know which rooms are the most prestigious ones?
- elaborate decoration, scale, views, location, grand approach route

■ How does the inside relate to the outside?
- are the important rooms the ones that the outside suggested?
- which rooms have the best views? Is this significant?

■ Have there been any alterations to the inside?

Removals? Why?
- disaster, redundancy, fashion, deterioration, cost
Additions? Why?
- fashion, new needs, increasing wealth, status symbol

■ What was the function of individual rooms? What is the evidence?
- public/private, specialized/general, status symbol

■ How do the rooms relate to each other?
- clear hierarchy, private/public, arranged in apartments/circles

■ What do the use and layout of the rooms say about how the house was used and about its owners? What do they say about the time in which it was built? What do they say about the people who have preserved them?

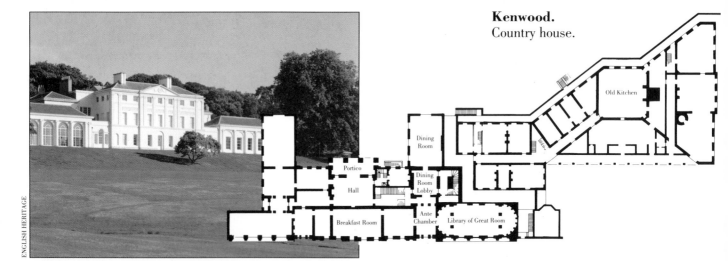

Kenwood.
Country house.

Victorian terraced house.
Domestic house.

	Kenwood Country house	**Victorian terraced house** Domestic house
Why has this house been built here?	**Observation** Good views. **Research** Fashionable countryside area near Hampstead within convenient distance of London. Clean air.	**Observation** Terrace follows line of railway. Part of development that includes grander square. **Research** Land became available for building in the early nineteenth century. Need for middle class housing for London's expanding population.
What building materials have been chosen? Why?	**Observation** Stucco (smooth cement render) for main part of house, probably red brick beneath. White Suffolk brick on later extensions. **Research** Stucco fashionable in the eighteenth century. Late eighteenth-century alterations were intended to look distinct and not blend in with earlier building.	**Observation** Yellow London bricks, some stucco, slate roof. Cheap but solid. **Research** Type of building material to be used was specified when land sold for building.
Are there signs of alteration outside? Why?	**Observation** From the north the brick wings stand out as additions to the central stucco core. Frieze (decoration at roof line) and string-course (decorative line at first floor level) do not continue on brick wings. Orangery and library wing do not match and were built at different times. Purple-brown bricks of service wing may be of different date to main core. **Research** Inside the Adam facade there is a seventeenth-century core but this is not obvious from observation.	**Observation** Cornice round bay, apparent in some of the rest of the terrace, missing. Outside lavatory used as a garden shed. Bay cornice too heavy to continue to support itself. Modern developer not concerned with continuity with rest of terrace. **Research** Preference for bathrooms and inside lavatories in second half of twentieth century.
What style has been chosen? Why?	**Observation** Neoclassical. **Research** Highly fashionable when changes made in mid eighteenth century.	**Observation** Plain Victorian terrace. Utilitarian.
How does the inside relate to the outside?	**Observation** Entrance portico related clearly to symmetrical entrance hall within. Principal rooms on south front with view over grounds towards London. Music room with verandah overlooks flower-garden. Relationship of interior to exterior lost in part in additional wings where some of the windows are sham.	**Observation** Bay at front of house marks principal room. Double windows on first floor mark main bedroom. Lack of symmetry inside reflected on outside.
How do you know which rooms are the most prestigious ones?	**Observation** The library has the most elaborate ceiling and fittings indicating fashionable cultured owner. Rooms on the south side, being originally the most public, have the best views.	**Observation** The front room has a marble fireplace, cornice and ceiling rose. It has a bay window and wooden shutters.
Have there been any alterations on the inside?	**Research** Alterations have occurred but this is clearer from documentary sources than from the site itself.	**Observation** The back has been divided and an inside lavatory and bathroom installed. New dividing wall plasterboard whereas all the others are brick. **Research** Doors have been changed because panelled doors became unfashionable.
How do the rooms relate to each other?	**Observation** Largely circular pattern in central core. Main apartments vertically divided. Rooms in wings interconnecting.	**Observation** Each entered separately from hall or landing, except for the front and middle rooms, and the breakfast room and kitchen, which interconnect.
What does the house say about its usage, owners, and the time it was built?	**Observation** Desire to impress and be seen from a distance. Use of grand house to indicate status. Contrast between formal north front and light-hearted domestic garden front. Need for homes for important people near London.	**Observation** Separation of sleeping and living. Provision of hot water system and internal bathroom and lavatory suggest increased concern with hygiene. Modest aspirations. Need for cheap solid housing indicates expanding population.

EMPTY AND RUINED HOUSES

Empty and ruined houses provide first-class teaching resources. Their educational potential is often undervalued because they appear difficult to use. It is only necessary, however, to develop a few transferable techniques to be able to unlock this resource for your pupils.

Such sites offer many advantages. Firstly, you will avoid the frustration of being unable to deviate from a one-way route round the house with no chance of doubling back to look again at something interesting. You will also be able to examine by touch, a method impossible in furnished houses, and the fragmentary nature of the remains means that building materials and techniques are more clearly apparent. Ruins lend themselves to the detective approach where pupils are asked to piece together evidence to support a particular view.

DOUBLE-CHECKING THE EVIDENCE

All evidence should be treated with extreme caution. Any house open to the public will have had at least two histories, the first as a home and the second as a monument or museum. Conservation alters things and it is almost as subject to fashion as architecture itself. Today the practice is generally to 'conserve as found' and not to make any alteration. This is not, in reality, possible. In order to halt deterioration, intervention has to occur. This is not always immediately apparent to the visitor.

The act of conserving a building changes it. At Appuldurcombe House, on the Isle of Wight, part of the building was roofed to protect it, and, to keep damp and pigeons out, the window-frames were replaced and the windows glazed. Walls often have to be capped to prevent water from infiltrating. Opening a building to the public may also lead to alterations being made; railings are put up or fire exits made for safety,

Appuldurcombe House, Isle of Wight, in 1947 after being taken into guardianship and before panelling and other additions were removed.

Appuldurcombe House in 1984.

Appuldurcombe House in 1989 after reglazing.

rooms are converted to lavatories or cafes, and areas that might otherwise become muddy are paved or covered in gravel. Interpreting the site to the public may also create anomalies. At Belsay Hall, in Northumberland, a room has been left with the floor boards up and the plaster partially stripped back to show construction details; when the house was a home no occupant would have seen it like this.

More radical alterations have

been made in the interests of conservation. In the 1950s and 1960s buildings were returned to a period of their history that was considered at the time to be of particular significance. This might have required removal of later additions. At Audley End House nineteenth-century alterations on the ground floor were removed to restore the basic layout of a Robert Adam suite. At Dover Castle a three-storey nineteenth-century barrack block was knocked down to save maintenance costs at a time when barrack blocks were not considered important. Often the end result of such changes is a twentieth-century interpretation which says as much about the interests and values of the twentieth century as it does about earlier architecture.

Chiswick House, London, is another twentieth-century creation. The house that stands today was built in the 1720s by Lord Burlington as a villa attached to an older house. Here guests were entertained and works of art displayed whilst more domestic activity occurred in the older house. The old house was demolished in 1788 and wings were added on either side of the villa containing more public rooms as well as new domestic offices. By the 1950s the house was empty and had fallen into disrepair. There had, however, been an increase of interest in the works of Lord Burlington, so a decision was made to restore only the parts that had been built by him and demolish the rest. The result is that today we see an arrangement that never existed when the building was a home. It is the entirely artificial creation of architectural historians.

Now, at English Heritage sites, there is an attempt to make the difference between old and new work clear. Nothing is ever faked up to look old, and new stonework is dated and sometimes a different colour stone is chosen to distinguish it. All may not be what it seems, however, and the message from these examples is that you should be very cautious about interpreting conserved buildings.

RECORDING THE BUILDING

One of the best ways to encourage pupils to observe a building carefully is to ask them to draw it. You may want a simple sketch plan or a more sophisticated record such as an elevation, a cross-section or a measured floor plan, or you may be asking for a personal interpretation that stands alone as a work of art. Whichever it is make clear what the purpose of the work is and how much

time is available. Provide good quality materials.

Select the media to match the intended outcome. Pencil and paper may be appropriate for a lengthy careful study. If you want to focus on architectural detail, prints done on polystyrene tiles give clear, bold and direct results. If the purpose is to record different architectural elements you could ask pupils to make a collage of those elements by choosing pieces of different-textured card and then making rubbings or prints from them. Classical architecture, with its pediments, columns, cornices and plinths, lends itself very well to this technique. Thick felt-tip pens may encourage pupils who are tentative about drawing.

Recording the exterior of a building can be turned into a collaborative exercise.

site by making a measured drawing of the ground plan. Depending on the age and experience of your pupils you could ask them to:

■ plot non-standard measurements (e.g. paces, shoe length) onto a plan

■ using a measuring rod, a click wheel or a 20 metre tape plot measurements onto a plan you have provided

■ draw their own rough plan with measurements marked on

■ make their own accurately measured plan of the site, or a part of it, using graph paper

Collaborative drawing of Bolsover Little Castle, Derbyshire.

ENGLISH HERITAGE

This method suits symmetrical buildings where bays repeat themselves. Plan the activity in advance of the class visit. Cut strips of paper of appropriate proportion and mark lines to indicate ground level, the roof line, and some other intermediate point, so that when the drawings are put together they match. The exercise demonstrates clearly how the repetition of certain elements creates a particular style.

Pupils can be asked to record the

Pupils can also be asked to record the elevation. They will have to measure along the base of the walls to plot the distances at which details occur. The height of the features can be estimated by looking at a child of a known height standing against the wall, and estimating how many times that child would fit into the space. Alternatively a clinometer could be used.

LOOKING FOR CLUES

Piecing together clues about life in the past from the remains of a building is a common archaeological technique. *Murder in the Billiard Room* is a variation of this type of activity which asks pupils to look at a site after a fictional crime has taken place. This is a motivating activity that you might like to try as an introduction to working with ruined or empty houses. Pupils are introduced to the concept of evidence and are encouraged to examine the building closely. They practise using a plan, find out about the layout of the house, and start to imagine the appearance of the house before it fell into ruins.

This version of the activity took place at Appuldurcombe House, on the Isle of Wight, an eighteenth-century ruin in a Capability Brown setting. Pupils were asked to imagine that there had been a tragic event at the house in the nineteenth century which had led to the house being abandoned (hence its present ruined state). A body was found in the billiard room. Pupils worked in small groups and were given a large brown envelope. This contained a ground plan of the house, a list of the witnesses, instructions, a chart for recording their findings, and a small envelope which contained five cards, one for each of the witnesses, printed with sections from the witnesses' statements. The pupils took on the role of the police, checking the truth of the statements by careful observation of the building. At the end of each round pupils returned to the teacher to collect the next envelope of statements. There were four rounds.

This type of activity works well because it is couched in the form of a game that everyone understands. Various adaptations are possible. You can make the activity more complicated by allowing each suspect one incorrect statement, explaining that in the heat of the moment recollection is not always clear. You could set the event at a specific date; any reference to parts of the building put up after that date would be excluded.

Once the murderer is denounced you could ask pupils to invent another suspect, decide their location at the time of the murder, and write four

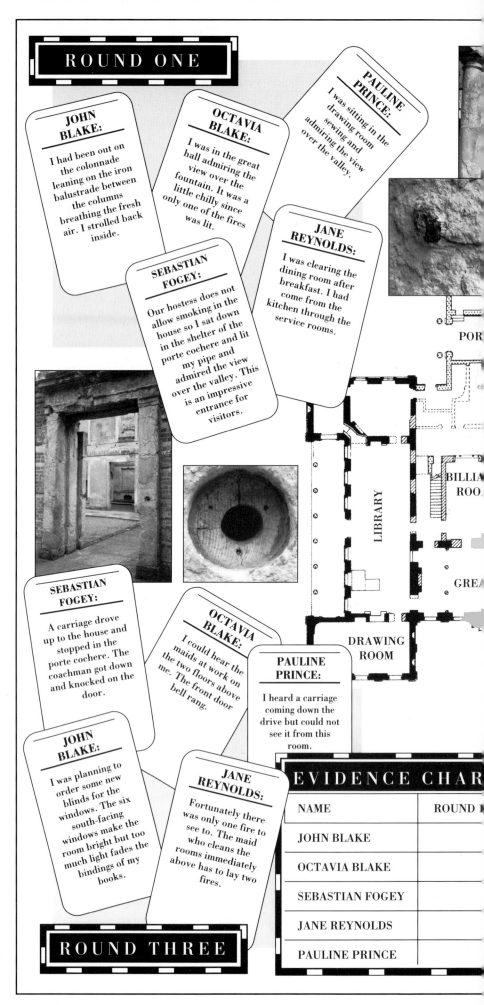

ROUND ONE

JOHN BLAKE:
I had been out on the colonnade leaning on the iron balustrade between the columns breathing the fresh air. I strolled back inside.

OCTAVIA BLAKE:
I was in the great hall admiring the view over the fountain. It was a little chilly since only one of the fires was lit.

PAULINE PRINCE:
I was sitting in the drawing room sewing and admiring the view over the valley.

SEBASTIAN FOGEY:
Our hostess does not allow smoking in the house so I sat down in the shelter of the porte cochere and lit my pipe and admired the view over the valley. This is an impressive entrance for visitors.

JANE REYNOLDS:
I was clearing the dining room after breakfast. I had come from the kitchen through the service rooms.

SEBASTIAN FOGEY:
A carriage drove up to the house and stopped in the porte cochere. The coachman got down and knocked on the door.

OCTAVIA BLAKE:
I could hear the maids at work on the two floors above me. The front door bell rang.

PAULINE PRINCE:
I heard a carriage coming down the drive but could not see it from this room.

JOHN BLAKE:
I was planning to order some new blinds for the windows. The six south-facing windows make the room bright but too much light fades the bindings of my books.

JANE REYNOLDS:
Fortunately there was only one fire to see to. The maid who cleans the rooms immediately above has to lay two fires.

ROUND THREE

LIBRARY

POR

BILLIA ROO

GREA

DRAWING ROOM

EVIDENCE CHAR
NAME	ROUND
JOHN BLAKE	
OCTAVIA BLAKE	
SEBASTIAN FOGEY	
JANE REYNOLDS	
PAULINE PRINCE	

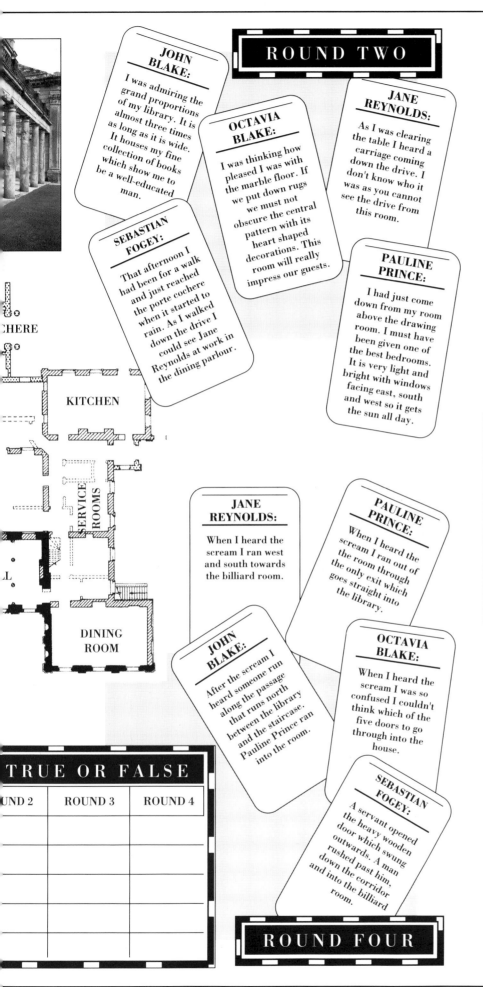

ROUND TWO

JOHN BLAKE:

I was admiring the grand proportions of my library. It is almost three times as long as it is wide. It houses my fine collection of books which show me to be a well-educated man.

OCTAVIA BLAKE:

I was thinking how pleased I was with the marble floor. If we put down rugs we must not obscure the central pattern with its heart shaped decorations. This room will really impress our guests.

JANE REYNOLDS:

As I was clearing the table I heard a carriage coming down the drive. I don't know who it was as you cannot see the drive from this room.

SEBASTIAN FOGEY:

That afternoon I had been for a walk and just reached the porte cochere when it started to rain. As I walked down the drive I could see Jane Reynolds at work in the dining parlour.

PAULINE PRINCE:

I had just come down from my room above the drawing room. I must have been given one of the best bedrooms. It is very light and bright with windows facing east, south and west so it gets the sun all day.

KITCHEN

SERVICE ROOMS

HERE

DINING ROOM

JANE REYNOLDS:

When I heard the scream I ran west and south towards the billiard room.

PAULINE PRINCE:

When I heard the scream I ran out of the room through the only exit which goes straight into the library.

JOHN BLAKE:

After the scream I heard someone run along the passage that runs north between the library and the staircase. Pauline Prince ran into the room.

OCTAVIA BLAKE:

When I heard the scream I was so confused I couldn't think which of the five doors to go through into the house.

SEBASTIAN FOGEY:

A servant opened the heavy wooden door which swung outwards. A man rushed past him, down the corridor and into the billiard room.

TRUE OR FALSE

...UND 2	ROUND 3	ROUND 4

ROUND FOUR

MURDER IN THE BILLIARD ROOM

Instructions

A body has been found in the billiard room. There are five suspects (everyone else in the house at the time has been ruled out). You are a detective. Your job is to find out which of the suspects is lying by looking for clues and evidence. Is there evidence against more than one person? Who are you going to take in for further questioning? The local chief inspector likes there to be proof of four lies before anyone is asked to help with enquiries.

These are the suspects and where they say they were at the time of the murder:

John Blake	Owner Library
Octavia Blake	Owner's wife Great hall
Sebastian Fogey	Guest Porte cochere
Jane Reynolds	Maid Dining room
Pauline Prince	Guest Drawing room

What to do

You have a plan of the building. Mark on it the place where the body was found and the place where each of the witnesses say they were at the time of the murder. You also have a chart on which to make notes of your suspicions. In the envelope there are extracts from the suspects' statements. Decide whether they are telling the truth and record your findings. When you have completed that round collect the next envelope from your teacher. There are four rounds.

Good sleuthing!

statements based on the physical evidence of the building. Putting the class's contributions together could lead to a completely different version of the game. Back at school the activity could lead to story writing explaining the events leading up to the murder or what happened next.

This basic idea can be adapted to a variety of houses but works best at ruined sites partly because you have to work at piecing together the clues about the building's history and partly because the fragmentary nature of the physical evidence stimulates the pupil's own deductive powers.

With some houses it might be possible to base the action round a real event. That this is a fictional murder does not create great problems since pupils are used to being asked to imagine things. It is important, however, that you check that they are clear where the border between fact and fiction lies and that you underline after the game what it is that they have learnt. Make the point very strongly that just as they were looking for clues so historians search for evidence about the past to piece it together.

UNDERSTANDING HOW THE HOUSE WORKED

The first chapter in this book showed how the layout of houses reflect the way that they are used and through this the values of the society that built them. Older pupils with experience of working at sites could attempt an analysis of a specific house in this way.

Ask pupils to work in groups so that they can try out their theories on each other. Give pupils an unlabelled plan of the house. Ask them to try to work out the function of individual rooms and to mark any significant features on the plan. Are there any signs that some rooms had higher status than others? Is it possible to identify the real, symbolic and psychological barriers within the building that controlled or arose from the relationship of the occupants? Are low ceilings, for example, or changes in the finish and materials of the floor or walls significant? The direction in which doors opened is sometimes important. Where a set of rooms is organized as an apartment the fireplaces generally face towards the entrance of that apartment. Is the

location of the water supply and drainage significant? Pupils should avoid reading the guidebook at this initial stage. Groups can then take it in turns to present their findings to the rest of the class.

A less sophisticated activity working with the same material would be to look at routes. Understanding the way a house was used requires an understanding of the different routes round a house. Give pupils a plan of the house and ask them to mark the routes taken by members of the household to do different activities. You will have to vary this according to the type of house, the areas on display, and the period you are dealing with, but useful roles might be a visitor being entertained for an evening, a servant bringing food to that guest, and the owner having breakfast and then dealing with some correspondence. Pupils could also try the exercise on their own homes as preparatory work to help them grasp the concept. Discuss where the routes coincided, which places were the most public and the most private, and who got to see the most splendid parts of the house. Discuss how these findings reflect social organization at the time the house was built or used.

Ask pupils to put together proposals for refurnishing the house. Use the site visit to make a plan of the house and to research other features. Is it possible to tell the function of individual rooms from observation? Is the location of fireplaces, windows, platforms or doors likely to affect the needs for and location of furniture? Back at school research the style of furniture appropriate to the house. Make sketches. Draw ground plans of each room to show where the furniture will be placed.

RECONSTRUCTING THE BUILDING

When a building remains only in a fragmentary state an obvious activity is to try to make a reconstruction of it as it might have looked at some fixed point in the past. You will have to choose your period with care and select the time for which the most evidence survives.

To help younger children translate surviving wall footings into a house

you could make a scale model, building up from the ground plan you have drawn. Using extant doors and windows as a guide to style, you could try to reconstruct the ruined

A Year 7 Expressive Arts Project
Brentford School spent half a term working on Chiswick House as part of an expressive arts course. They visited and drew parts that interested them. They were asked to write poetry that reflected their personal responses to the house and grounds and to prepare rhythms and movement that reflected it too. They visited the house again for a rehearsal and then on the day of the performance the top years of their feeder primary

ENGLISH HERITAGE

bits of the building, perhaps colouring the speculative bits of the model differently from those parts known to be accurate. Research on pictorial sources for the house may

schools were invited to come as an audience to see their work. The event started with a massed performance outside the house with the girls standing and moving in the shape of the house. A Chiswick House rap was performed and then the girls divided into groups at chosen points in the house where they danced or mimed events in the house's history. There was an exhibition of their art work in the garden where good use was made of the hedges and vistas to display their work.

provide evidence of the missing bits. Where there are many identical windows, doors or other shapes, you could take the best on-site drawing and reduce it to scale on a reducing photocopier and then reproduce it the requisite number of times to create a degree of uniformity in the model.

With some houses it is important to be able to recognize different architectural styles in order to work out the sequence of change. This is probably best tackled in school as preparation and then reinforced at the site. Develop matching exercises by collecting pictures of buildings from magazines and postcards. You could cut out features that then have to be returned to the appropriate building or you could prepare cards for sequencing exercises.

PERFORMING

It is possible to use historic houses simply as a backdrop and pupils could act out a play based on an event that had occurred at the period of the house or on something known to have happened to an occupant of the house. You might prefer, however, to devise an activity that uses the house more, and forces observation and understanding of the material remains of the past. Having worked out the function of some of the rooms pupils could be asked to bring them to life by creating tableaux showing those rooms in use. This might be a suitable activity for a secondary school and its feeder primary schools to collaborate over, with the older pupils planning the tableaux and the primary pupils acting as audience. It would need the support of the house manager whom you should approach at the planning stage.

USING CAMERAS

If you want to develop fresh approaches to a house it is sometimes useful to introduce some kind of constraint. Obliging pupils to use an item of equipment other than a piece of paper can sometimes jolt their thinking into new channels.

Check first that there is no objection on the part of the site owner to the use of a camera. This generally presents no problems outside (although it may inside where

considerations of security, copyright or conservation have led some houses to ban photography). The trick in thinking up a task based round a camera is to devise something that the pupils can do for themselves which requires thought, planning and discussion before any shutter release is pressed. Here are some ideas for the use of a camera.

It is sometimes difficult to get much of a sense of the people who lived in a house. Spend some time looking at a house together and concentrate on the image the owner wished to present. Look, too, at how the house reflects the roles of the other people who lived there. Were they insignificant people who were tucked away in basements or far courtyards, were they guests who had to be offered the best, or were they people whose support was needed? Ask pupils to select contrasting parts of the building and pose at a doorway in the roles of the different people who might go in there. They should demonstrate the contrasts by their demeanour.

Alternatively tell pupils that the owners of the site want to extend their postcard selection by adding four new exterior views, or details that most typify the house/display the contrasts between the differing building phases/show clues about previous uses, or whatever fits best with the strengths of the house you are dealing with. Working in a group they should plan their views and prepare captions for each.

A video camera can provide the same sort of motivational stimulus as an ordinary camera and, similarly, it should be the pupils who are behind it, not the teacher. Using a video requires much more time and skill than a similar exercise with a camera. Ask pupils to research and make a short documentary about the style of architecture of the chosen building. Alternatively they might prepare a short news report about an event, such as the building of a new wing because of the anticipated arrival of the monarch or the introduction of a new and fashionable style, relevant to the chosen building. Since it is the planning stage that is critical to the project's success, introduce the idea of a storyboard. Ask pupils to plan out their film by noting in sequence the shots they want together with the accompanying commentary or dialogue.

FURNISHED HOUSES

A visit to a furnished house is often chosen by teachers in preference to an empty one because it appears easier to use and gives pupils a better impression of life in whatever period is being studied. Historic houses open to the public are not, however, a neutral historical source. By being opened to visitors they have often lost their original function (home) and taken on a new one (museum). In the previous chapter we dealt with the problem created by the conservation of the building.

Here we look at some of the problems related to the furnishings.

You need to know something of the previous history of the house in order to understand the display. There are different types of house to spot:

The continuously occupied house
If a house has been in occupation continuously over many decades or centuries then the furnishings will have been built up over the years too. Sometimes a grand new scheme of interior decoration may have led to the wholesale replacement of furniture in some rooms with something new, but often a large number of periods will be reflected. This in itself causes difficulty, especially with younger children, who need to be able to recognise a single style before being able to spot variations. Examples: Castle Howard, Yorkshire; Penshurst Place, Kent.

The refurnished house Some houses have had their original contents destroyed or dispersed. The

Changes at Osborne House

Look closely at the photograph of the drawing room at Osborne House in 1876 and compare it with the same room in 1981 to identify the changes that had taken place. The carpet and chandeliers have gone and some of the ornaments are different. Additional furniture was included in the 1980s and it was differently arranged. There was a roped-off walk-way.

Why did these changes occur? They are a reflection of the changing use of the house. In 1876 the house was still Queen Victoria's private home. In 1904, after her death, Edward VII gave it to the nation and today it is a museum. The specially fitted carpet may have been worn away or removed, like the chandeliers, to another royal house or palace. In the twentieth century the needs of conservation and the tourist compete. The walk-way allows for the heavy flow of visitors and the furniture was crammed up behind the ropes.

What do these photographs tell us about the societies that produced these rooms? The different arrangements of the furniture are significant. In 1876 the furniture was well-spaced as befits one of the more public rooms of the house where nobody sat without the permission of the Queen. The room reflects the status of its owner. The 1980s arrangement of the chairs in a cosy circle by the fire was partly caused by the need for space for the visitors but was it also an unconscious reflection of our own image of family life? Were twentieth-century expectations imposed on a room originally designed and used to reflect another set of values? Rooms reflect the ideas and assumptions of their time.

Drawing room at Osborne House, Isle of Wight, in 1876.

Drawing room at Osborne House in 1981.

furnishings there now may have been collected as specific examples of what was there before. They will not, however, be the same, and no conclusions should be drawn about the house's previous history from those furnishings. Examples: Marble Hill House, Twickenham; Boscobel House, Shropshire.

The reused house Many local authorities are faced with having to find new uses for historic houses that have outlived their original function. In the past the solution has often been to create a historic house museum. Sometimes these houses have been used to display furniture that has already been acquired. The practice here has often been to arrange it in period rooms with no intrusions from earlier dates. Where there are large collections of pictures the house is sometimes converted to what is essentially a gallery with perhaps a few pieces of furniture dotted about.

Examples: The Geffrye Museum, London; Strangers Hall Museum, Norwich; Christchurch Mansion, Ipswich.

The reproduction house Another approach, faced with an empty house, is to work from an inventory and other surviving evidence and have replicas made to try to reconstruct the interior exactly. This approach may be used where the building is of major historical importance. Examples : Medieval Merchant's House, Southampton; King's Apartments, Hampton Court Palace.

The combination house Many houses use a variety of the last three approaches, which you should attempt to disentangle. At Ranger's House, for example, some of the rooms are reused as picture galleries, some as straightforward museum displays of a collection of musical instruments, and some are set out according to eighteenth-century inventories. Some rooms follow one inventory, and some a later one. Examples: Kenwood, Hampstead; Audley End House, Essex; Kensington Palace.

Even where the contents of a house are substantially intact you need to be extremely cautious about accepting that the house looks today as it always looked. Lighting, heating or paint finishes may have changed, and fabric will have faded

or rotted and been replaced over time. Twentieth-century taste determines what historic houses look like just as much as it determines our own homes.

Floors are a classic example of this. We have a preference for highly polished boards in historic houses. In fact many floors were covered with painted oilcloths but since these were not highly valued they were thrown out when worn and only fragments survive. In the eighteenth century when floors were left bare it would have been normal to polish an inlaid floor to bring out the colour and the grain, but for plain boards the usual treatment was dry scrubbing.

Those who manage historic properties have to make judgements about the display of houses. Decisions have to be made about the date to which a house will be returned. Contents tend to be weeded so that it is extremely unusual to see a 1960s coffee table in amongst eighteenth-century furniture, whereas this might have been quite feasible in somebody's home.

It will be clear from this that no furnished house can be taken at its face value and something of the history of its collection together with curatorial judgements need to be known or deduced.

INTERPRETING THE EVIDENCE

Older pupils should be quite critical of what they see and they should be able to recognise that a historic house is not a neutral source of history but a curator's interpretation.

Prepare pupils for analysing a historic house by looking at their own and other people's homes. What can you tell about people from their rooms? What tasks and values are reflected in their rooms? How do people use their possessions to present a particular image of themselves? Pupils could try to extend this analysis to spaces used collectively such as a classroom or assembly hall. How are the values of the school given a physical presence? They could photograph their own bedroom and write an article about it, or their friends could make an analysis from the photo.

ENGLISH HERITAGE

Replica fourteenth-century furniture at the Medieval Merchant's House, Southampton.

TOPHAM PICTURE SOURCE

At the house allocate groups of pupils to different rooms. Ask them initially to record what they can of the lives and aspirations of the people who lived there. Then ask them to think again about the display and to identify any judgements that the curator has had to make. Whose lives are being interpreted? What are the gaps in the evidence? What interpretive techniques have been used? Do they trust the interpretation? What more might they need to know?

One of your aims in visiting a house might be to give pupils the opportunity to learn about furniture of a particular period at first hand. Again drawing will help observation. Younger pupils might like to be given a tightly defined task with a clear outcome.

The understanding of style is partly to do with recognizing shape. The silhouettes of Tudor and Georgian furniture, for example, are

The Observer Magazine ran a series of articles called 'A room of my own' in which famous people described their favourite rooms.

fundamentally different, and making a shadow theatre may be a good way of helping children recognize these differences. Make the front of the theatre by cutting a rectangle from the middle of a large sheet of card. Cover this hole with tracing-paper to make the screen. Check that pupils understand what a profile is. Tasks could be divided between pupils. Some could draw profiles of furniture whilst others record costume outlines from portraits. Some could record the details of fireplaces and lighting. Some could draw the silhouette of the building itself. Transfer outlines onto thick black sugar paper and cut out the shapes. You may want to have everything drawn to scale or it might be better just to make sure children

know what size screen their cut-outs have to fit within. Set up the screen with the beam of a projector shining through it from the back. Fix a length of wire to each silhouette so that children can hold their cut-out between the light and the screen without their bodies getting in the way. Experiment with different scenes. The ambitious could improvise a short story or do scenes of different periods.

PROBLEM SOLVING

There are a variety of teaching methods that go under the heading of problem solving. For the purposes of this section we define it quite closely. It refers to putting pupils in role so that they are obliged to look at a problem through the eyes of another person. In this case we have chosen to look at historical material through present-day eyes. For example: Habitat want to bring out a range of fabrics inspired by the house you are visiting. You are the designer. Go to the house and make a record of some of the designs you see there on the building and in the furniture. Note colours that are frequently used at the house. Select three ideas to offer to the fabric buyer and show how they could be turned into fabric designs.

There are certain features of the problem that you should notice. First of all it is the activity rather than the frame that is important. It does not actually matter whether pupils are a Habitat designer or not. What matters is that they look carefully at designs and colours used in the house. The frame is simply there as an embellishment that helps motivate the pupil and provides both focus and boundary for the study. Secondly, the frame can be discarded. Because you looked at the problem of design through the eyes of a Habitat designer does not mean you have to continue to do this, but when the frame is discarded the information acquired through the frame is retained. Details of design and fabric will remain to be used in other contexts such as a study of the style of the period.

Here are some sample problems that you may be able to adapt for the age range and house you are working with:

■ Next's new mail order catalogue is enormously successful and they have decided to expand their range of frames and mirrors. You have been asked to

ENGLISH HERITAGE

Shadow puppet theatre made at Aston Hall, Birmingham

provide some sketches based on traditional designs. Make a selection of four possible frames from X House and prepare the drawings for the Sales Director.

■ You are doing the picture research for a book being written by a psychologist on facial expression. You still need to find examples of candour, relief, smugness, confidence and indifference. Can the pictures, sculpture and tapestry at X House help you?

■ The tea room is being decorated and a new location has to be found for it for the next six months. The curator is anxious about spoiling the display. Which room could you clear for it without diminishing the visitor's experience? How could the new decorative scheme reflect the house? Produce an illustrated report for the curator.

■ Following the fire at Hampton Court a few years ago the manager of X House is very concerned about fire risks. What are the exit routes from this area of the building? The warding staff are going to be given training for dealing with a fire. Once they have cleared the building of visitors which item in each room should they rescue first? Prepare a report for the house manager.

Problem solving is an ideal activity to set as group work. The approach requires selection, prioritization or decision-making. Pupils are forced by their peers to justify their choice and support their arguments, and can subsequently bring a better thought-out view to whole-class discussions.

Devising your own problems can be quite difficult at first but gradually you will find they come more easily. The following rules will help you. Always decide first what it is you want your pupils to look at. Devise the frame to go round that focus rather than thinking up the role or frame first. Modern frames to look at historical problems work better than trying to think up historical ones. Avoid being over prescriptive; once you have identified the problem do what you can to avoid telling pupils how to solve it. The value of this activity is that they can come to their own solution themselves. Trial and error will show how much guidance is necessary.

LANGUAGE WORK

Historic houses offer opportunities to practise using different forms of writing for different purposes. Old houses and their gardens may be tranquil or atmospheric. They are often used to inspire poetry writing. Since it can be hard to begin ask pupils to start by making a collection of appropriate words suggested by the site. Imposing a constraint may help. Ask pupils to compose lines of poetry with a stated number of syllables. In this example, done on an INSET course, groups were asked to write a poem with the following pattern of syllables: 1,3,3,3,3,3,3 or 1,5,7,7,7,7,7 or 5,5,5,5,5. Their work was put together to make the shape of the house.

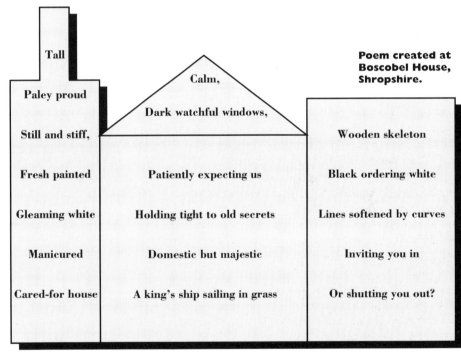

Poem created at Boscobel House, Shropshire.

Tall
Paley proud
Still and stiff,
Fresh painted
Gleaming white
Manicured
Cared-for house

Calm,
Dark watchful windows,
Patiently expecting us
Holding tight to old secrets
Domestic but majestic
A king's ship sailing in grass

Wooden skeleton
Black ordering white
Lines softened by curves
Inviting you in
Or shutting you out?

Other kinds of writing can be produced. Obtain a copy of estate agents' particulars for a local house or keep cuttings from the press. Look at these together in class and observe the choice of vocabulary, the conventions used, and the generally positive tone. Ask pupils to prepare their own particulars for the house being studied.

There was a vogue in the eighteenth century for writing satirical verse. Sometimes it featured houses. Here is an epigram from Lord Hervey on Chiswick House:

Possessed of one great hall of state,
Without one room to sleep or eat,
How well you build, let flattery tell
And all mankind, how ill you dwell.

This was Jonathan Swift's offering on Marble Hill House:

My House was built but for a Show
My Lady's empty Pockets know;
And now she will not have a Shilling
To raise the Stairs or build the Ceiling.

Some South-Sea Broker from the City,
Will purchase me, the more the Pity,
Lay all my fine Plantations waste,
To fit them to his vulgar taste.

Pupils could be asked to compose their own poem about the house they have visited using the same rhyme scheme.

THE GROUNDS

When Humphry Repton wanted to explain his ideas to a potential client he produced a Red Book, so called because he put together comments, plans and watercolours in a red, leather-bound volume. A feature of these volumes was the flaps attached to the paintings that allowed him to show before and after views. He painted the grounds as they looked and then parts of the scene lifted to reveal how they would look after improvement.

ENGLISH HERITAGE

ENGLISH HERITAGE

Pages from a Red Book showing the original view and **Repton's design drawn onto an overlay flap.**

bamboo canes and sellotape to support the work once in place. If everyone is clearly briefed at the outset it is possible to carry out an ambitious project in a single visit.

USING TAPE-RECORDERS

Hand-held tape-recorders are ideal for use in furnished historic houses. You will not run into the security and conservation problems that cameras sometimes create and they are a good way of making quick records when a house is crowded with visitors.

Where a room has been the scene of a famous event ask pupils to go to the room and make a radio report of that event, filling in the detail so that the listeners at home have a vivid picture of the scene. This will require considerable preparation as pupils will need to know the background to the event and the people involved as well as to have thought about the nature of on-the-spot reporting.

A group could prepare an edition of the old style 'Down your Way', interviewing different members of the household in the rooms they most frequently occupied. Alternatively pupils could be asked to provide a tape tour of one room or group of rooms for a visitor with a visual impairment.

THE SERVANTS – A POSTSCRIPT

For many teachers the life of a servant is the topic of study that occurs to them first. Children can understand what servants did and are interested in it, and teachers often feel that the study counterbalances the upper-class bias of the historic house. You should, however, think very carefully before you opt for this line of approach. Many houses do not display the domestic offices because they were either swept away long ago or what survives is of a much later date than the rest of the house. Reconstructing them leads into the dilemmas outlined at the start of this chapter. If you take this line you will often be opting to work with negative evidence. It is, of course, appropriate to look for what is missing and to ask why this is the case, but this may make a better classroom discussion than a focus for a visit.

You could produce a class Red Book. Discuss the ways in which a landscape might be improved. Use a pre-set paper size and ask pupils to work in landscape format. You could provide a base drawing with all the key features of the current landscape roughed in or you could ask pupils to start from scratch. Get them to complete the scene as it is today and on a second sheet to sketch roughly the improvements they would make. Back at school plan out the work carefully to make lift-up views. Every pupil should write an explanation of their suggestions just as Repton did and all contributions should be bound together in a red-covered volume.

Small-scale formal gardens often relied for effect on views and vistas terminated by a feature such as a sculpture, pillar or temple. Ask pupils to study these features and to record them by drawing or photography, close up and from a distance. Note their scale and the devices like paths or hedges that draw the eye towards them.
Ask pupils to find a view that could be improved by a feature. Record the view and then design an appropriate feature. Using large sheets of stone-coloured sugar paper and thick black felt-tip pens, draw and cut out the feature and then place it in the landscape and record the new view. Go prepared with string, scissors,

PICTORIAL AND DOCUMENTARY SOURCES

There is a large range of historical sources that help illuminate the study of a historic house and if you become enthused by one particular house you could build up a great many resources. This chapter concentrates on some of the more common or easily available types of source and looks particularly at how you can use them when you conduct a visit to the house. Written documents can present a certain difficulty. It is easy to find things to do with them in the classroom but sometimes the documents and the study of the house itself become two separate but parallel studies. This section suggests ways of making the studies converge.

You can spend an enormous amount of time looking for appropriate documents for a specific house and then become despondent when inevitably it turns out that what you want has not survived. Try not to let this put you off. There are two possible courses of action: either you can confine yourself to using what is available or you can find a way of using a document from a similar type of house. Make your choice clear to your pupils .

VISUAL SOURCES

Maps and plans

The Ordnance Survey was founded in 1791 to prepare a one inch/mile map of Great Britain. The one inch maps are too small scale to be useful for the study of individual houses, but the introduction of the six inch survey in 1840 and the twenty five inch survey in 1853 was much more helpful. It is possible to see the development of a site and to date changes with some accuracy, although it should be remembered that the date of surveying may be several years before the date of publication.

You might choose to give pupils extracts from a run of maps before a visit. Ask them to write a history of the site from this and list things that have been altered or demolished to see whether any evidence remains. Maps can also be used after the visit to explain features that were observed.

Plans were produced for all sorts of reasons. For houses from the mid nineteenth century onwards there may be original architects' drawings or you may find plans drawn up when an alteration was proposed. Auctioneers' inventories sometimes include a plan and at some sites plans were drawn up as part of a set of instructions for the staff. You may be able to use plans to identify the function of rooms in the past or to interpret the details of an alteration.

Prints and paintings

Large houses may have been the subject of series of prints in the eighteenth and nineteenth centuries and earlier. It would be worth looking to see whether Samuel and Nathaniel Buck, for example, visited in the early eighteenth century, because they made large clear pictures that are very suitable for use with pupils. You may also find large oil views or more intimate amateur watercolour interiors. You could try out the following activities:

Change over time Find the same view today. On a large blown-up copy of the print mark with a coloured pen all the changes that have occurred since the picture was made. Try to explain the reason for these differences.

3-D views If you can find a print of a site with a clear foreground, middleground and background, try this idea. Make three large copies of the print. Retain one whole. From the second cut away all the background leaving the middle and foreground. On the last print retain only the foreground. Now colour the prints and paste them upright on a base each a little in front of the other to make a 3-D view of the building. At the site prepare a set of three similar drawings to show how the site looks today.

Photographs

Many large houses have at some time had sets of photographs taken of their interiors. These may have been done to celebrate the opening, redecoration or new use of the building, or they may have been to record it for publication or archive purposes. Subject, angle, and mood will all be influenced by the reason for the photo and it is important to try to see if you can establish what this was.

Sharpening the focus To help pupils to look carefully at a photograph give them a magnifying glass. Alternatively cut out a small cardboard frame of the right proportion to help see exactly the same view as in the photograph.

ENGLISH HERITAGE

Watercolour of the saloon at Audley End in 1853. Much of the furniture has case covers in place.

Pupils could use cameras to take the same view for comparison back at school. (Check that photography is permitted.)

Curators for a day Tell pupils that they are curators whose job it is to restore an interior to the way it was at the date of a specific photograph. This activity will raise a number of issues. How do they know what was behind the photographer? Is there any reasonable way of working it out? Will they have to remove anything from display? Is this a good idea? What will they do with those things? How are they going to replace things that are missing? Are they going to use replicas? What difference will that make to the display? They can either write a report on their proposals or be asked to make some drawings, plans or elevations to indicate their proposals. This could perhaps culminate in a debate on whether it is preferable to leave the display as it is or attempt a restoration.

Forgotten views Sometimes you will manage to find only photos of rooms that either no longer exist or are not open to visitors, or whose plans or contents are so altered as to be unrecognizable. This need not discount their use during a site visit. Depending on the room you might ask pupils to see if there are sufficient items round the house that could be brought together to reconstruct that room.

Photographing a room Your class could try photographing their classroom, the staffroom, the head's office or their own bedrooms with a Polaroid camera to see the difficulty of including all the significant features. Allow them to settle on the most appropriate shot and to move some items if necessary. If several groups work on this independently the results can be compared.

Peopling the house Peopling a building requires an imaginative leap that can be aided by the use of

Photographs as historical evidence

Question the value of photographs as historical evidence for the arrangement of rooms. Look at the picture of the drawing room of Walmer Castle in 1919. Does it give an accurate impression of the appearance of the castle at that date? It helps if you know why a picture was taken. Was it to make a social point, was it to record a special event, or was it, as in this case, to make a record for a fashionable magazine? Consider whether the contents were specially rearranged for the photographer. Was the furniture always like this with a single elbow chair drawn up to an empty hearth and the card-table set cornerwise to the fire? Were cards actually played, in which case what did the players sit on? Were the surfaces generally more cluttered? Had they been cleared especially to give a more ordered classical look? Today the reverse seems to occur. A casual glance at The World of Interiors or other style magazines shows a clutter of decorative objects that move in each new shot and that sometimes seem to have been brought in from other rooms to add to the fashionable assemblage.

Consider how prevailing fashions and the purpose of the photograph may have influenced its content and mood and thus the historical message.

COUNTRY LIFE

Walmer Castle drawing room in 1919.

NATIONAL TRUST

photographs. This photograph of Frank Green and his servants sitting outside the Treasurer's House in York in about 1925 is typical of the formal photographs often associated with historic houses. Frequently, as in this case, there are no domestic quarters on display today. It is still possible, however, to make good use of this picture on a visit. You can identify the role of most of the people in this photo (butler, footman, housekeeper, chef and housemaid for example). At school children could adopt a character, giving them a name if their true names are not known, and research the type of work that servant was expected to do. The task at the site would be to go round those parts of the house that are open looking at them through the eyes of that servant. What work would they have to do in which rooms? What difficulties would there be? What routes would they have to take? (Check that key areas are not out of bounds and that the visitor route round the house does not make this activity too complicated.) What would they be carrying? Which other servants would they be working with? They could perhaps try to estimate the length of time each activity would take. They might imagine the course of a day there. Back at school they could hold a conversation in role between some of the servants on, for example, Mr Green's plans to introduce the vacuum cleaner, or write an application for a job, or work out what equipment would be needed in the domestic quarters and research their detail.

Children could adopt a person and build up a life story and a family using a combination of imagination and research. They could visit the house in role imagining they were a guest, a tradesperson, a villager or an applicant for a job (try governess or chaplain). Alternatively they could use the visit to further their research into their subject's choice of house style and furniture and costume. Older pupils, who have made a study of the sorts of evidence that historical photographs provide, could use the visit to compare their findings with the differing evidence provided by buildings and their contents.

WRITTEN SOURCES

Inventories

Of the written sources associated with houses one of the most useful is the inventory. The main types are:

Probate inventories After someone died the Church held the monopoly over settling their affairs. An administrator was appointed who had to make an inventory and present it and an account to the Church within a specified period. The inventory lists all the moveable possessions of the dead person. Inventories go back at least to the thirteenth century but the period from which survivals are most numerous runs from 1660 to 1750. They cover belongings such as houses, furniture, clothes, livestock, crops, tools, stock, ready money, money due and money owing. Often possessions are listed room by room.

Insurance inventories These largely date from the nineteenth and twentieth centuries and list all major items for insurance purposes. You may find that people are unwilling to let you see or use a modern one for fear of highlighting current values and attracting theft.

Auctioneers' inventories These generally date from the nineteenth and twentieth centuries. When an estate came up for sale an auctioneer would list the lots. Major lots might be land and buildings but sometimes a day of a sale might be devoted to the house contents which would often be listed by room.

Curatorial inventories Museums keep registers of all the items belonging to the museum and curators of a historic house prepare a list of the contents of each room either as a record for their own purposes or sometimes with explanatory notes as an aid to the visiting public. You may be able to get copies of these in advance of your visit.

Frank Green in the garden of the Treasurers House, York, with his servants in about 1925.

Inventory for Ranger's House, 1728

This is an extract from the probate inventory of Ranger's House drawn up in 1728 following the death of its occupant Admiral Francis Hosier. Spelling and punctuation have been modernised. The original is in the Public Record Office.

In the large Stone Hall

Item a large and a small mahogany table, four green Windsor chairs, a steel stove complete, a pair of glass arms [candle holders], a large glass light with crimson lines, tassels and pulleys, a picture in a black frame, all the India paper as framed in five black frames, two mahogany tables, a coat of arms in a black frame.

In the Crimson Camblet Parlour

Item three sets of crimson camblet [fabric made from wool and silk mix] window curtains, valence, rods and window seats, six walnut tree chairs with red morocco leather seats, one round and one square mahogany table, a large pier [tall mirror, often set between windows glass] in a gilt frame 48 by 28, top 30 by 28, a chimney pier glass 43 by 27, end 27 by 7^{1}/$_{3}$ and a pair of double brass branches [candle sticks], a stove and furniture complete, and hearth brush, a marble table with iron brackets, four coverlets for a carpet.

In the Green Silk Damask Parlour

Item a field bedstead [day bed] with green silk damask furniture [upholstery] and counterpane and with a case of green silk complete, feather bed and bolster, chequered mattress, and white holland quilt, three blankets, three sets of green silk damask window curtains, valence, cornices and rods, one elbow chair and four backed stools, India backs and pincushion seats covered with damask, and cases of serge, a square walnut tree table, a dressing glass, another with drawers 22 by 13, a chimney glass in a gold and glass frame 43 by 27, ends 27 by 7, a pair of

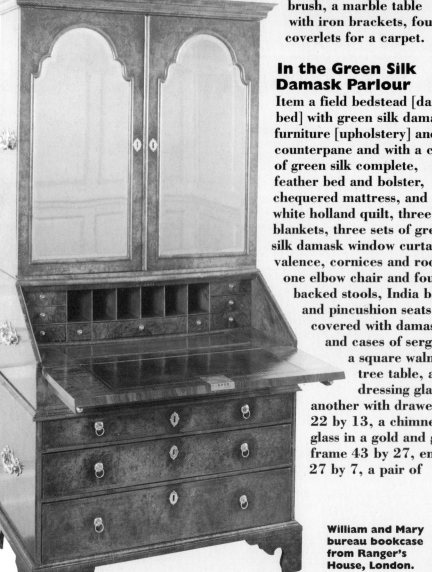

William and Mary bureau bookcase from Ranger's House, London.

double brass branches, a picture in a gilt frame, a steel stove and furniture complete and hearth brush, five pieces of green damask hangings containing fifty yards.

In the Large Dining-Room

Item three sets of crimson silk damask window curtains, valence, cornices and rods, a couch and squab, three pillows ditto with cases of serge to them, two settees with walnut tree frames, the seats covered with red morocco leather, ten chairs ditto, a walnut tree card-table, two marble tables, silvered frames, two pier glasses, silvered and glass frames 51 by 31, ends 31 by 25, a steel stove, shovel, tongs and poker, a pair of double silvered branches, a large silvered branch with crimson silk line and tassel, four coverlets for a carpet, a glass case and a frame for the model of a ship, one brass cannon.

In the Little Dressing-Room

Item two sets striped silk window curtains and rods, two luted and two matted chairs, a small carpet, a chimney glass, walnut frame 25 by 20 … 20 by 7, a pair of brass arms, a steel fender, a marble table on iron brackets, six prints in black frames.

In the Common Parlour

Item a stove and furniture complete, hearth brush and pair of bellows, a chimney glass in walnut tree frame 38 by 18 ends 18 by 18…a pair of brass branches, a sconce in a walnut tree and gilt frame with two branches 34 by 24… one eight-day clock in a walnut tree case with chimes and weather glass, an easy chair and cushion, six matted chairs, a card-table, a round mahogany table, a carpet.

What can you do with inventories? First check whether the rooms referred to are open to the public. If they are, check the contents of the inventory against the contents of the rooms. Attempt to match the inventory with what survives. This may have to be done selectively with a large document. Are there any reasons why certain items have survived and not others? How full a picture does the inventory give of the life of that house or person? Is the source biased? What has been omitted?

Once you have worked through the inventory the activity you select will depend very much on individual circumstances. The rooms listed on the Ranger's House inventory are all on the ground floor. A useful exercise is to ask pupils to imagine that the house is empty and that by using the inventory they have to decide which room is which before they start to furnish them. There are two particular problems that have to be solved. Firstly, the number of windows and curtains do not appear

to match, but when students remember that a new room was added after the date of this inventory then it becomes clear that windows were lost when new building butted up to what was previously an outside wall. Secondly, two rooms appear interchangeable. But once pupils find that the person who drew up the inventory went round the house in a logical sequence then that problem too is solved.

If a room is not on display or no longer exists this need not stop you using the inventory at the house. Try

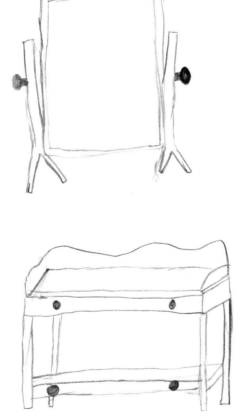

Child's visual inventory of a room at Boscobel House, Shropshire.

to recreate the room from the inventory by research. Draw a plan, a diagram or a perspective view as it might have looked. Younger pupils may like to create a shoe-box model. Is there any evidence in the rooms that survive to help you? Look carefully at the furniture and pictures on display. Does this give any clues about how the room might have looked? Any deficiencies could be made up by further research in reference books in school.

If the room and the inventory match to a certain extent pupils could be asked to check the contents against the display. They could be asked to record discrepancies and suggest reasons for these.

Where room and inventory match exactly this can result in very tedious matching exercises. You could ask pupils to devise some way of recording all items in place including pictures on the walls. This could result in the development of a net.

A curatorial inventory could be used to help explain the work of the house manager. Pupils could be given an inventory to study for one room then asked to prepare inventories of the rest. They could be given reference books to help them find the appropriate vocabulary. Alternatively pupils could be asked to make a visual inventory of another room.

A page from the 1861 census showing Osborne House when Queen Victoria was in residence.

Census returns

The census was first taken in this country in 1801 when the threat of a Napoleonic invasion concentrated the government's mind on Britain's human resources. It has been taken every ten years since then (with the exception of 1941) and provides an excellent source for the study of houses. The key documents are the ennumerators' notebooks which are available from 1841 to 1891 after which time the 100 year confidentiality rule applies.

Here is a sample page from the 1861 census for Osborne House, Queen Victoria's private home on the Isle of Wight. The census provided a record of who was at home on a designated night. If the owners of the house were away on that particular night then the conclusions about their household will be rather different.

Census returns are a rich source of historical evidence opening the way to small-scale surveys (most popular first names, family size, or occupations) or large computerized analyses. They work best in relation to a visit, however, if you can find

some way to make the link between the written document and the physical remains of the household listed.

An extract from the census for your house allows children to find out about real named people who lived there. Each child could take one person and try to find out about them. With some houses it might be possible to find out the detail of their life history but it is more likely that you will only be able to guess at that, and instead the classroom activity might be to use reference books to try to find out what sort of life they would have had: their education, work, family, and leisure activity. On the visit to the site pupils could look at the house from the point of view of that person and perhaps try to imagine a day at home for them. The task could be to write a diary entry.

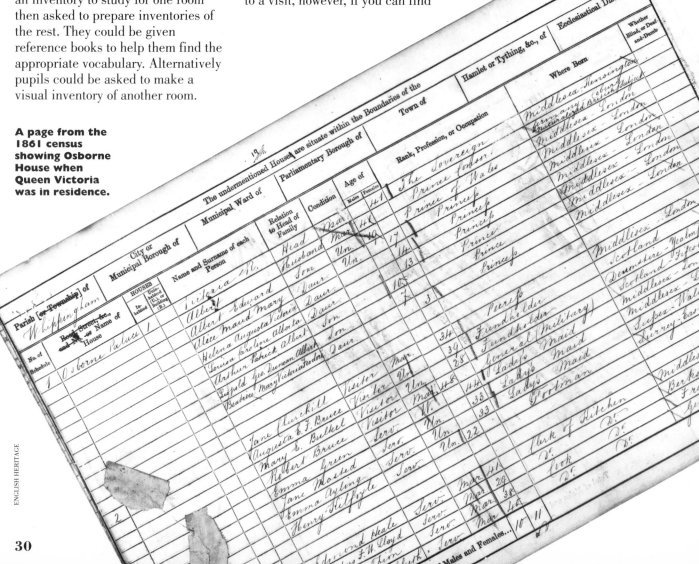

ENGLISH HERITAGE

HISTORIC HOUSES TODAY

It is not essential to study historic houses in their historical context. There are ways of looking at them in their present contexts that bring many benefits. Two current issues worth looking at are conservation and tourism.

CONSERVATION

Country house visiting goes back to the late seventeenth century but this occurred under the strict supervision of the housekeeper and parties were very limited. As interest developed some owners started to issue tickets and rules.

On your visit you might want to warn your class against seeing with their fingers, a form of behaviour that infuriated Horace Walpole at Strawberry Hill:

'Two companies had been to see my house last week, and one of the parties, as vulgar people always see with the ends of their fingers, had broken the end of my invaluable eagle's bill, and to conceal their mischief, had pocketed the piece... It almost provokes me to shut up my house, when obliging begets injury.'

Some teachers get very frustrated trying to use historic houses with their pupils. They understand the very real value to children of being able to touch things and yet the furnished house with its roped walkways and warding staff is designed to stop this.

Unfortunately this cannot be otherwise. Our historic houses are fragile and vulnerable and were never intended to take the wear from visitors that their increasing audience gives them today. Delicate textiles were never meant to be exposed to the light for so long and we are often unaware of the extraordinary care that used to be taken in the past to protect them.

In 1776, the newly married Susannah Whatman, aware that gilding is fragile and that the sun rots and fades fabric, wrote a book of instructions to her servants:

'The sun comes into the Library very early. The window on that side of the bow window must have the blind let down. The painted chairs must not be knocked against anything, or against one another. The books are not to be meddled with, but they may be dusted as far as the wing of a goose will go.'

ADAM HINTON

Preparing for the day's visitors at Blenheim Palace.

From the seventeenth century it was customary for all fine seats to be supplied with one or two sets of covers, known as case covers, to protect the main upholstery on less formal occasions. Gilded furniture might have chamois leather stockings to protect the legs, and extra sets of curtains to protect bed and window hangings and tapestries were not unusual. Wooden furniture that might fade was provided with leather and baize covers, and sometimes covers were provided for carpets as well. This level of care makes it still possible to look at fine items in historic houses. We face the dilemma that through opening houses we are hastening their decay and yet we can often only justify their continued existence by keeping them open to all.

Even the heat from the bodies of visitors can be harmful. One person emits as much heat as a 100 watt light bulb and at heavily visited sites the fluctuations in temperature caused by hundreds of people during visitor hours may cause expansion and shrinking that can separate oil paint from a canvas or split panelling.

If the buildings and their contents are to survive into the foreseeable future then protecting them as much as possible from light, dust, humidity and temperature change is essential.

Since you will find the evidence of wear and tear and efforts to combat this at all historic houses, especially the furnished ones, this makes an excellent area of study for pupils.

Take this opportunity to teach children about the difficulties and issues of conservation. At the site ask children to look for examples of wear and deterioration and their causes: rubbed paintwork, damaged curtains where visitors have yielded to the temptation to finger a rich fabric, worn carpets in doorways, objects broken by careless handling, stonework damaged by atmospheric pollution or subsidence. Look for ways in which damage is limited: smoke detectors, burglar alarms, barriers, glass cases, rolled carpets, low lighting, bans on flash photography and stiletto heels.

31

Pupils could work in groups to produce a conservation audit for the house. Can they identify any particular threats to the future of the house and do they have any suggestions for change?

You could prepare for the visit by thinking about the way materials deteriorate. Take a clean white piece of cloth, cut it in two and ask your pupils to pass one piece round the class three times. Compare its condition with its pair. Ask pupils to devise some other tests. Find examples of iron, cloth, paper, wood, glass and pottery. Bury these in the school grounds and dig them up in, say, six weeks' time. Look for deterioration and discuss.

The culmination of your work on conservation could be a debate. A suitable topic might be: Historic houses should only open one day a week to protect their contents for future generations.

TOURISM

Visiting historic houses is an important part of the leisure industry. A survey was carried out in 1988-89 of all leisure day visits of three hours or more, excluding those from a holiday base. It estimated that the whole population of Great Britain made 1,684 million day trips annually. About 1% of trips each were to stately homes (9 million visits), museums and art galleries (13 million visits), and theme parks (12 million visits), and the chart on the right provides information about those visits.

Your pupils could conduct a survey to see how far the house you are studying conforms to the national pattern of visiting. Ask them to identify the information they need and devise a questionnaire. Test this on class members before using it on the public. You should obtain permission from the site to do this project and you should ensure that pupils work in groups of not less than three and observe the normal rules for personal safety. Discussion of the results could raise debate about the differences between visitors at stately homes, museums and theme parks.

Pupils might make a study of the facilities available at a particular house. Again, discuss the possibilities before the visit and devise a report

form to use at the site. You might like to put children in role for this activity. They could be a firm of marketing consultants whose job it is to make recommendations to increase income or visitor numbers. Alternatively they could be asked to look specifically for facilities for a particular group like families or the retired. Back at school use computers to generate graphs and statistics to put in their report. Artists'

Do they complement the site? Could pupils design better ones? Are instructional signs clear? Are they negative and unwelcoming? Pupils could be asked to plot signs on a plan of the site and come up with a better scheme.

Looking at how the historical information is put across is quite a sophisticated task and you might find it easier to concentrate on a single room or group of rooms than to

Leisure day trips

	Stately homes	Museums	Theme parks
Length of trip (expressed as a percentage of total visits to that type of site)			
less than 10 miles	5	18	32
10-29 miles	35	27	33
30-49 miles	13	15	12
50+ miles	47	40	23
Duration of trip (expressed as a percentage of total visits to that type of site)			
3-4 hours	20	20	2
4-5 hours	17	18	12
5-6 hours	25	12	16
6+ hours	38	50	70
Expenditure (expressed as a percentage of total expenditure on visits to that type of site)			
fuel	16	11	11
fares	10	17	7
admission charge	14	17	37
food and drink	29	28	32
gifts	14	17	7
other	17	10	6

The information on this chart has been adapted from Dodd, T, **Leisure day visits 1988-89**, Office of Population Censuses and Surveys, HMSO, 1991, ISBN 0-11-691358-4.

impressions of improved facilities would also be useful.

Historic houses open to the public often aim to put across a certain amount of information. Pupils could be asked to look at the information systems within the house or grounds that tell people what to do or give historical background. At a large site directional signs might be worth assessing. How is it done, does it work, and could it be improved? Is the design of the signs appropriate?

attempt the whole site. Ask pupils to plot the visitor route on a plan and to record any interpretive materials. Can they think of any better way of informing visitors? Could they convert written information into graphic material, for example, or devise an information board for a room that currently has no explanation? Could they produce an audio tour? Any method devised could be tested on members of another class.

MAKING THE MOST OF YOUR VISIT

A really successful visit will have taken account of both social and curriculum needs as well as addressing the practicalities. This section looks first at some organizational matters and then addresses the links between visits to historic houses and the curriculum.

ORGANIZATION

There are some particular features of historic house visiting that you should take into account:

Preparation of accompanying adults Since one-way routes round furnished houses are common and your party is likely to be broken up into smaller groups, it is especially important that the accompanying adults are well prepared. Hold a meeting, write briefing notes, or use the journey to explain your aims to your helpers. Provide them with a little background history to the site. Discuss the activities you have planned and explain how you want pupils to work. Accompanying parents may need some prompting to see that it is often better to help a child arrive at their own answer than to supply the answer for them.

Supervision No matter how old your pupils are, never leave them unsupervised in a furnished house.

One-way routes Where there is a one-way system round a house that is liable to overcrowding, avoid preparing a worksheet that requires pupils to find and record specific objects. You will clog up the route and create friction with other visitors and warding staff. Make sure any activity you set coincides with the route and does not require doubling back. Where there are narrow corridors be sure that you have a member of staff at the back and the front of your party.

Guided tours Guided tours are available at some historic houses. If these are optional you should think very carefully whether this is what your pupils need. Go on a tour yourself and get a sense of the content of the tour. Have the guides been trained and are they sensitive to school visitor needs? Do you think they have the ability to work with a class from your school? Think about why you are going. If it is to train your pupils in powers of observation and deduction then it may not be appropriate to start with someone who may either tell them all the answers or set their own agenda.

Conservation Stress the importance of not touching things and explain the reason why. If you are using clipboards train pupils to hold them underneath and warn them against leaning on furniture or glass cases. Bulldog clips scratch furniture and it is preferable to secure paper to board with rubber bands.

Slack periods At busy houses warding staff may be instructed to keep visitors moving. It is worthwhile to ask the administrator when the slack periods are and to fit your visit in at those times.

Preliminary visit It is essential that you (and if possible your colleagues) make a planning visit to the site.Even if you have visited the house before you are recommended to do this as routes may have changed.

Education centres Many houses are beginning to provide special facilities for school parties. Is there a room that can be used as a base? Find out how it is equipped, how long you can book it for, and whether you are allowed to eat packed lunches there.

Warding staff. Warding staff are employed first and foremost for security and secondly as sources of information. In some places they may be actively discouraged from engaging in conversation with visitors as the potential thief or vandal will wait for just such an opportunity to pounce. Warding staff have enormous experience of school parties and appreciate groups that are well prepared. Their expectations are often a reflection of their own experience at school. Children with heads buried in worksheets are often seen as the ideal. You do not have to conform to these expectations but you should be aware of them. Some heritage organisations are realising the key role of warding staff and putting considerable effort into staff training.

THE CURRICULUM

A study of the historic house will serve most areas of the National Curriculum.

History

The programmes of study in KS 2 are the most obvious place where the study of historic houses falls in the History curriculum. It is relevant also in KS 3 and 4 where the study of architecture and culture is required. At KS 1 children learning about the past can start work from the familiar concept of home, and having looked at a historic house start to discuss similarity and difference.

Historic houses and their contents are sources of history. Pupils will start to understand that they provide different but complementary information to documents. By working at a house they will also start to understand that there are particular methods which can be used to elicit information from it which can tell us about the people and society who made it, lived in it and kept it. What may be less obvious is that any house which has been altered in order to open it to the public is an interpretation of history and therefore a useful area of study in contrast to written sources.

Maths

The study of architecture requires an understanding of shape and of symmetry. Tessellation can be seen in use in the decorative schemes of many houses. Surveying and measured drawing requires the practical application of many mathematical skills. Younger children can be asked to look for specific shapes such as circles, squares, triangles or rectangles. The language of maths can be used to describe a route or a ceiling pattern.

English

The opportunities to follow the English curriculum at a historic house are enormous. Many activities require considerable discussion and debate to arrive at a solution. Different types of language are used at sites (instructional notices, narrative text in the guidebook, conversational style on videos or brief provision of information on labels and inventories) from which you could develop work.

Science

The conservation aspects of the historic house require the investigation of materials and their properties. Making structures requires the application of physics. Earth sciences and the study of plants and insect life can be developed in the grounds.

Technology

There are two major areas in which the historic house serves the interest of the technology curriculum. Firstly, throughout the curriculum there is a stress on looking at the solution of design problems in other times and other places. Secondly, the curriculum requires a study of information systems. Historic houses attempt to manage the visitor experience and put across a certain amount of information. The effectiveness of these systems can be studied and improved solutions can be proposed. You might set a project to build a doll's house based on a historic property.

Art

Historic houses offer pupils an opportunity both to develop a knowledge and understanding of art by study of the wide variety on display, and also, through the activities set at the site, to investigate and make things using the rich visual stimuli to inform their own work. Pupils might be required to design a poster or a guidebook cover or produce a set of postcards.

Music

Historic houses can provide a historical context for the study of music. Pupils can find out about the types of music that might have been played in the house in the past or they can use the building and grounds to inspire their own work. Their task might be to create sounds and rhythms to accompany a video of the house.

Geography

Pupils can develop their geographical skills by using or producing their own maps and plans of a site with date keys. They can make the house part of a study of their own locality and judge the house's influence on local settlement, the economy and the environment.

CROSS-CURRICULAR THEMES

Careers education and guidance

There are many different careers available in historic houses requiring varied levels of educational attainment. You may be able to arrange some on-site interviews.

Personal and social education

As citizens pupils will need to have a view on the appropriate use of public money and on how they may wish to spend their leisure time.

Multi-cultural education

Large historic houses are sometimes thought of as tricky because they represent a single culture. In fact this perception can be broken down because they are excellent places to demonstrate that culture in England is an amalgam of many cultural influences from Greek architecture through Far Eastern ceramics to Indian textiles and based on wealth from Africa. It is hard to enter a furnished room in a historic house without coming across items and ideas from other cultures.

Health education

Some houses can provide a historical context to work on personal hygiene through a study of sanitation and the provision of heated or running water.

Gender issues

If you embark on drama and role play with mixed classes at historic houses, keep a check on who is playing the exciting, active roles and who the passive ones. If the purpose of role play is to develop empathy for people with whose lives you are unfamiliar, there is no reason why boys always have to take on male roles and girls female ones. Recent studies have shown the key business role played by women in medieval and later merchant families. Victorian women, who were often forced into particular domestic roles, had considerable management responsibilities, either as the lady of a large household or as a housekeeper. Given a well-documented house you might be able to make a study of the gender roles within it and then look to see how these are reflected by the house itself. Were any areas associated with a specific gender? Were the furniture and fittings designed differently? Greek revival furniture in the early nineteenth century, for example, was used for male rooms because its design was seen as bold, unfettered and strong.

Economic awareness

At a large house you could look at the division of labour amongst the workforce or you might be able to work on historic accounts. Considering the financial priorities in caring for a large stock of crumbling historic houses might create more impact.

Environmental education

Issues of conservation are central to the study of historic houses and their gardens.

RESOURCES AND BIBLIOGRAPHY

LOCAL SOURCES

The house
The first place to start is at the house itself. Find out who is responsible for the historical aspects of the building; they may have relevant documents and pictures or be able to tell you where these are kept. Make contact well in advance of starting the work with pupils.

Reference or local studies library
Find out which of your local libraries maintains a local studies collection. This will have a wealth of secondary sources and may also keep a collection of old pictures.

Local museum
Local museums may contain related documents. Since not all material will be on display it is worth asking curators if they have relevant material in store.

County Record Office
For primary documentary sources such as inventories, for maps, plans and possibly census returns, the County Record Office will be a key source. Contact the archivist well in advance of a visit since research facilities are often heavily booked.

NATIONAL ORGANISATIONS
English Heritage has a photographic library that covers its own sites. It deals with postal and telephone enquiries as well as personal visits, for which an appointment should be made. Contact:
The Photographic Library
English Heritage
Fortress House
23 Savile Row
London WlX 1AB
Tel: 071-973 3338

The National Building Record is run by the Royal Commission on the

ENGLISH HERITAGE

Historical Monuments of England which was started in 1941 to collect records of historic buildings threatened or already damaged by bombing. There is a large photograph collection covering the whole of England and arranged in box files by county and civil parish. Enquiries can be made by post, telephone or personal visit. Contact:
National Building Record
Fortress House
23 Savile Row
London WlX 1AB
Tel: 071-973 3091

The National Trust opens 190 houses to the public and offers corporate membership to schools. Contact:
Education Officer
National Trust
36 Queen Anne's Gate
London SWlH 9AS
Tel: 071-222 9251

The Royal Institute of British Architects has an extensive library. Contact:
The Education Officer
Royal Institute of British Architects
66 Portland Place
London WlN 4AD
Tel: 071-580 5533

BIBLIOGRAPHY

History of houses
Ayres, J, **The Shell book of the home in Britain: decoration, design and construction of vernacular interiors, 1500-1850,** Faber & Faber, 1981, ISBN 0-571-11625-6. Good on details like floor coverings and window design in modest houses. Information in accessible form not easily found elsewhere.

Brunskill, R, **Illustrated handbook of vernacular architecture,** Faber and Faber, 1987, ISBN 0-571-13916-7. Good on details of buildings, extensive photos, sketches and maps. Useful appendix with methodology for studying buildings.

Davidson, C, **A woman's work is never done; a history of housework in the British Isles 1650-1950,** Chatto and Windus, 1982, ISBN 0-7011-3901-3.

Fowler, J and Cornforth, J, **English decoration in the eighteenth century,** Barrie and Jenkins, 1978, ISBN 0-214-20552-5. A useful survey explaining how and why furniture was designed and arranged. Includes information about housekeeping.

Girouard, M, **Life in the English country house: a social and architectural history,** Yale, 1978, ISBN 0-300-02273-5. This is the key volume on understanding the use and layout of the historic house and has been a great influence on the ideas in this book.

Hewison, R, **The heritage industry: Britain in a climate of decline,** Methuen, 1987, ISBN 0-413-16110-2. A critical view

35

of the type of conservation that distorts and sanitizes our history.

Summerson, J, **Architecture in Britain,** Penguin 1991, ISBN.0-14056-1785

Thornton, P, **Seventeenth-century interior decoration in England, France and Holland,** Yale, 1978, ISBN 0-300-02193-3. A thorough study showing how information can be pieced together from prints and paintings.

Tinniswood, A, **A history of country house visiting: five centuries of tourism and taste,** Basil Blackwell/The National Trust, 1989, ISBN 0- 631-14801-9. Whatman, S, **The housekeeping book of Susannah Whatman,** Century/The National Trust, 1988, ISBN 0-7126-1755-8.

Documents

Cox, N and J, 'Probate inventories', **The Local Historian,** 16(3), August 1984 and 16(4), November 1984. Explains historical background and outlines contents.

Miller, S T, 'The value of photographs as historical evidence', **The Local Historian** 15(8), 1983. A short and useful discussion of the points to be aware of when considering photographs as historical evidence.

Steel, D J and Taylor, L, **Family history in schools,** Phillimore, 1973, ISBN 0-900592-60-5. Worth trying to get hold of even though now out of date. Practical chapter on using photographs.

Stephens, W B, **Sources for English local history,** Manchester University Press, 1973, ISBN 0-7190-0505-1. Useful reference book.

The educational use of the historic house

Adams, E and Ward, C, **Art and the built environment,** Longman/Schools Council, 1982, ISBN 0-582-36195-8. Full of interesting ideas, especially for secondary school art, but applicable more widely.

Copeland, T, **A teacher's guide to maths and the historic environment,** English Heritage, 1992, ISBN 1-85074-329-0.

Durbin, G, Morris, S, and

Wilkinson, S, **A teacher's guide to learning from objects,** English Heritage, 1990, ISBN 1-85074-259-6. Suggests a method of analysing objects and a range of classroom games to help develop the skills that are necessary for fieldwork.

Ellsworth, L F and Ellsworth, L V, 'House-reading: how to study historic houses as symbols of society', **History News** (USA) 35(5), pp 9-13, 1980. Suggests a methodology for the study of houses.

Fairclough, J and Redsell, P, **Living history: reconstructing the past with children,** English Heritage, 1985, ISBN 1-85074-073-9

Keith, C, **A teacher's guide to using listed buildings,** English Heritage, 1991, ISBN 1-85074-297-9. Many large country houses are listed and this book covers the issues related to listing and conservation and suggests activities to bring out these points.

Morris, S, **A teacher's guide to using portraits,** English Heritage, 1989, ISBN 1-85074-231-6. Shows how to analyse portraits and suggests classroom and on-site activities.

Pownall, J and Hutson, N, **A teacher's guide to science and the historic environment,** English Heritage, 1992, ISBN 1-85074-331-2.

Schlereth, T J, 'Historic house museums: seven teaching strategies', **Artifacts and the American past,** American Association for State and Local History, 1980. Sophisticated lines of approach for undergraduates.

Steane, J, **Upstanding archaeology** [buildings], Council for British Archaeology, Archaeology for Schools series, 1985. An archaeologist's view of buildings concentrating on close observation of materials and methods of building and recording plans and elevations.

Books for children

Gee, A, **Looking at houses,** Batsford, 1983, ISBN 0-7134-0845-6. A very useful look at individual features, with good diagrams. For secondary pupils.

Swift, K, **Homes,** Longman, 1991, ISBN 0-582-04018-3. Introduction to historical sources at KS 1.

Whitlock, R, **Exploring buildings,** Wayland, 1987,

ISBN 1-85210-002-8. Ideas for a local project for pupils in KS 2 and 3.

Audio Visual

The archaeological detectives, English Heritage, 20 minutes. Two primary pupils investigate three very different historic sites, including Appuldurcombe House.

Clues challenge, English Heritage, 14 minutes. Two children visit a modern location familiar to them and apply detective skills which can be developed on later visits to historic sites. Basic clues are sought about a furnished house, an empty bungalow and a building site.

Living history, English Heritage, 21 minutes. Outlines for teachers the various stages of setting up and carrying out living history projects at sites and at school.

Boscobel House, English Heritage, 10 minutes.

ACKNOWLEDGEMENTS

We are very grateful to the following people for help in producing this book: David Anderson, Carole Mahoney, Mary Mellors, Susan Morris and John Reeve.